HOW TO STOP SELF SABOTAGE

An Athlete's Guide To Removing Non-Serving Behaviour, Thoughts, Emotions and Feelings

RACHEL BINETTE

Foreward

This short book - the third in the Mindset Rx'd series - was written by Mindset Rx'd Coach, Rachel Binette. Coach Rachel is a Certified CrossFit Level 3 Trainer, and a writer. She is a contributor to Breaking Muscle and a foundational part of the Mindset Rx'd Team.

Mindset Rx'd is the world's first scaleable mindset system for functional athletes. We have worked with elite athletes at The CrossFit Games® as well as hundreds of non-elite athletes. We are on a mission to provide effective and practical mindset coaching to every box-member worldwide, should they need it, so the athlete can become the best version of themselves possible - in fitness and wider life too.

COACH RACHEL

Introduction

I remember as a young student putting off until the last minute every assignment I was given. I was constantly stressed about deadlines, but never did anything in order to give myself more time to complete papers.

On the swim team, I intentionally held back from truly racing, whether in training or during swim meets.

More recently, I was standing at our kitchen window, looking out at the backyard while the dogs played in the grass, and when I looked down into my hand, I was eating a cookie. How did that get there?

And many more times, I have reached for my phone and opened Facebook or Instagram or YouTube, when I knew I should have been writing, researching, or studying.

Many of us ask ourselves, why do we do the things we do?

Why can't I get myself to go the gym?

Why can't I stop overeating and stick to a nutrition plan?

Why can't I sit down and study the way I know I need to, in order to pass the test?

Why can't I convince myself to apply for the job I know I want?

Why can't I do the things I say I want to do?

Most would say that we have poor willpower, that we don't "want it bad enough." Our rational minds love this explanation. I'm too weak-minded, too scared, too stupid, too fat. I'm not good enough to get what I want.

The fact is, those behaviours that we refer to as non-serving (overeating, skipping the gym, procrastinating, etc.), are all the product of **Bound Nature**.

Before we dive into Bound Nature and it's associated self-sabotaging behaviours, let's look at it's opposite: **Free Nature**.

(Bound and Free Nature are terms originally introduced to Mindset Rx'd by Mindset Rx'd founder, Tom's, mentors, Brian Grasso & Carrie Campbell. Without these two, Mindset Rx'd wouldn't be here, and our eternal thanks goes out to their pioneering nature and benevolence).

Free Nature

Free Nature is the state we are born into. Uninfluenced, pure.

Think about a well-fed baby.

They are present. Content. Open. What's more, they feel this way even if - especially if - obstacles arise. This is Free Nature.

How often do you find yourself in a mental state that is this clear, open, and content? Have you ever been in flow, that state of complete absorption in an activity that makes time seem to slow down? How often are you focused on the present moment, rather than what was or what could have been?

When we are anything but present, content, absorbed in what we find meaningful, and open, we are in Bound Nature.

When we obsess about the past or the future, when we're frustrated, disappointed, angry, sad, fearful, or anxious, when we behave in ways that are self-destructive (ranging anywhere from procrastinating to substance abuse), it is our Bound Nature that is creating conflict.

Through Free Nature, we experience gratitude, creativity, and quiet confidence. Free Nature is, quite simply, our best self, when all is flowing and we are content.

Where does it all go wrong?

The Origins of Bound Nature

Behaviours

We usually notice Bound Nature first through non-serving behaviours - all of those things we say we want to do, but cannot seem to, or those behaviours that we keep on doing even though we want to stop.

It is not a lack of willpower or the wrong type of goal setting that causes us to self-sabotage. Along with the behaviours that draw us away from our goals, are thoughts and emotions that self-sabotage us.

Thoughts and Emotions

Self-sabotaging thoughts lead to our behaviours.

Before we decide to skip the gym, we think,

"I'm too tired."
"It's fine to miss it this once."
"Later."
"It's not making a difference anyway."

And along with those thoughts are emotions: frustration, guilt, anxiety, fear, impatience.

Our emotional state is difficult, if not impossible, to change at will; if anyone has ever told you to "stop being sad," you know well that to stop feeling is not possible. We require either a resolution to the problem that is causing our emotions or a shift in perspective.

The only way to resolve an emotion is to understand its source, and the source of our emotions and the thoughts that accompany them are our beliefs.

Beliefs

"Whether you say you can or you can't, you are right." - Henry Ford

"Can" or "can't" are just the tip of the iceberg when it comes to the beliefs we hold about ourselves, about our place in the world, and what the world is like. The stories that we've created to make sense of why we are the way we are, why the world is the way it is, and why our life in particular is the way it is (as well as what it could be or should be), have influenced our thoughts and emotions, and in turn, our behaviours.

Mindset work is focused on uncovering our subconscious beliefs and examining them: does this belief serve me anymore? Can I choose another perspective on myself or my place in the world that serves me better?

Before we uncover our subconscious beliefs, it is beneficial to understand where those beliefs originated from: where our Free Nature turned into Bound Nature is through our influences.

Influences

Our Free Nature is uninfluenced, like the baby in the introduction. A baby has basic needs that must be met, but when those needs (food, sleep, physical contact, shelter) are fulfilled, a baby is in Free Nature.

An uninfluenced nature is one that does not hold beliefs. Babies do not "believe" in anything: they simply exist in the present. They behave in ways that are biologically wired into their behaviour to have their needs met (crying when they are hungry, for example), but a baby does not "believe" that crying will lead to feeding.

As we grow up, we experience influences, and these influences contribute to our beliefs.

Educational. What we are taught by those we trust influences our beliefs.
Environmental. What cultures we experience influence our beliefs.
Experiential. All experiences have the potential to influence our beliefs.
Evolutionary. Our biology, particularly brain development, influences our beliefs.

Educational

Our educational influences include everything that we are taught explicitly. This includes our schooling, what we're taught to believe in religion and spirituality, etc.

Environmental

Environmental influences are the things we are taught implicitly. What country we grow up in, how our culture views the elderly, illness, gender roles, how our parents raise us, and much more contributes to our environmental influences.

Experiential

Our experiences are another influence on our beliefs, but this is more complicated than it seems. It is not only our experiences that influence us, but our perspective on our experiences, and the perspective we take is often something that has been taught to us through our environment.

Take, for example, a child who has been bitten by a dog (for our purposes, the bite is only a nip, not a severe injury). A child can interpret this experience in many ways:

When a dog is growling at me, I might get bitten.
Dogs are dangerous, I might get bitten.

Through one perspective, a child sees a warning signal and has learned to heed the warning to avoid future accidents. In the second perspective, the child has learned that all dogs are dangerous and will now avoid all dogs. How do we develop such different perspectives? Our environment.

A child regularly exposed to discomfort, who is self-reliant, will typically react to experiences of minor discomfort with confidence. A child who is sheltered from discomfort will lack self-confidence when discomfort eventually finds them, and will typically react to experiences of discomfort as a victim.

Evolutionary Influences

Our evolutionary influences hold great sway over us and there are several we could cover here, but the main one that can contribute to Bound Nature is our negativity bias.

Negativity Bias

We are wired to respond to negative input from our senses more strongly than neutral or positive input. Storing a negative experience in memory takes milliseconds and happens subconsciously, where storing a positive experience requires a dozen or more seconds of conscious attention. That is exponentially more work! The reason is that negative experiences are more important for our survival to remember than positive ones. Our biology doesn't care if we're "happy," it cares that we remain alive.

Our experiences, our environment, our education, and our evolution all contribute to the beliefs that we develop as we grow up, and these beliefs are what influence our behaviour. By the time we are adults, our beliefs have become subconscious, and the thoughts, emotions, and behaviours that stem from them have become automatic, relegated to our subconscious mind.

While most non-serving behaviours are not as dramatic as self-mutilation or addiction, all non-serving behaviours are a type of coping mechanism for discomfort. At one point in time in our lives, these Bound Natures and their accompanying behaviours, emotions, and thoughts were serving us. It's only when they are no longer needed but have become subconscious that we find ourselves scrolling through Instagram, skipping the gym, or overeating as though in highway hypnosis, unaware of what we're doing until we've already arrived on the other side.

How do we begin to break this cycle?

By understanding our own Bound Natures.

Bound Nature Examples

Behaviours

- Procrastinating.
- Avoiding conflict.
- Saying yes to too many things.
- Holding back ideas.
- Avoiding discomfort, staying in comfort zone.
- Overeating or undereating.
- Skipping the gym, mobility, or recovery.
- Cherry-picking workouts.
- Short-changing reps.
- Ignoring injuries.
- Chasing too many goals at the same time.
- Inconsistency.
- Yelling, overcompensating with aggressive, intimidating behaviour.
- Giving up.
- Withdrawing socially.
- Becoming distracted.

Thoughts

- "I can't do this."
- "I don't have time."
- "Why me?"
- "Bad things always happen."
- "I never get the same opportunities as other people."
- "No one understands me."
- "It's different for them."
- "This hurts."
- "This is hard."

- "I'm going to be last."
- "I'm slower/weaker than everyone else."
- "Everyone is watching me."
- "I'm better than them."
- "I need to be better."
- "I should be better."

Emotions

- Despair.
- Anger.
- Frustration.
- Sadness.
- Overwhelmed.
- Insecurity.
- Loneliness.
- Jealousy.
- Mistrustfulness.
- Impatience.
- Blame.
- Fearfulness.
- Apathy.
- Aggression.

Physical Sensations

- Heaviness.
- Tiredness.
- Exhaustion.
- Weakness.
- Resting bitch face.
- Lack of eye contact.
- Racing heart.
- Shallow breathing.

- Flushed face.
- Chronic pain.
- Chronic muscle tension.
- Hyperactivity.
- Inability to be still.
- Shoulders slumped, poor posture.

Creating Bound Nature Roles

Creating self-knowledge around our Bound Natures in all of their complexity is critical for mitigating their effects on our thoughts, emotions, and actions.

If we want to stop overeating, we have to understand why we do it. If we want to become more consistent in our gym attendance, attack training with more intensity, or stop procrastinating, we have to understand what has been holding us back so far.

Creating Bound Nature roles gives us the self-knowledge that allows us to stop our self-sabotaging behaviours before they begin. The word "role" is an important one: when we are in Bound Nature, we are acting a part, playing a character that is separate from ourselves.

When we earn the understanding that allows us to separate ourselves from our Bound Natures, we can stop our self-sabotaging behaviours before we perform them.

Step One - Observation and Organisation

Every Bound Nature has a physical presence, an emotional presence, and a behavioural presence, as outlined in the Bound Nature examples above. When experiencing any bound nature, write out what physical sensations, what emotions, what thoughts/words/phrases, and what behaviours occur together.

-How does the Bound Nature look? What do others see when you're in this BN, and what do you see?

-How does the BN feel, both physically and emotionally? Tiredness, weakness, and heaviness are common symptoms of BN.
-What are the emotions this BN expresses?
-What does the BN sound like? What does it say? What type of language does it use? What does this BN think of you and your place in the world? What does it think about other people?

Each set of behaviours and the accompanying physical sensations, emotions, and thoughts are their own Bound Natures. Every one of us has dozens of unidentified BN, but typically we experience a top 2-5 BN that have the greatest impact on our lives. Observe and then organise these into roles.

Step Two - Separation

Give each Bound Nature role it's own name.

Visualise the person you become when you're in this BN. What is the body language like? What clothes do they wear? What tone of voice do they use?

Write all of this down. This is a big part of separating our Free Nature from our many Bound Natures, being able to visualise this role as separate from our free nature.

For example, I have a Bound Nature called:

THE PERFECTIONIST

Sounds like: "What are you doing?" "What is wrong with you?" "You are so stupid." "Ugh."
Feels like: Wound up, frazzled, distracted. Angry. Frustrated. But not surprised.

Looks like: Irritated, rolling eyes, throwing up hands in disgust.

Triggered by: Making mistakes, especially at work.

Behaviours: trying to fix things too quickly, trying to make others happy over myself, general focus on how others perceive me over how I perceive myself. Saying yes too much.

One of my clients has a Bound Nature called:

THE EARLY QUITTER

Sounds like: "There's no point." "Whatever." "They're better than me." Makes excuses.
Feels like: Apathetic.
Looks like: Eyes down, poor posture. Socially withdraws.

Triggered by: Discomfort. Comparisons.

Behaviours: doesn't push intensity in WODs, gives up on nutrition, other goals.

These BN roles are well organised now, but it took many pages and many sessions of writing over the course of months, as well as experiencing this BN multiple times, in order to flesh them out fully. We may yet have more to learn about these Bound Natures.

Step Three - Consistent Assessment of Bound Nature vs Free Nature

Once we have observed, organised, and gained separation from a Bound Nature, it is up to us to consistently assess whether we are in FN or BN, to decide whether a reaction in BN is warranted, or whether there is a better way.

This is the step that leads to ending self-sabotaging behaviours. It does require that we make mistakes along the way and that we learn from them.

As an example, I was aware of my perfectionist tendencies when beginning a new job, yet was unaware that the constant constructive feedback I was receiving was being taken in by The Perfectionist, rather than by my Free Nature. This led to me performing my job in a way that was designed to make my boss happy, to fear making mistakes so much that I held back the best parts of myself, to nearly quit because I was convinced I would never "get it right," and to generally push away my instincts. These were a difficult few months that culminated in a near breakdown, but they were necessary in order for me to recognise the deep impact, the hold, that this BN has over me.

Only because of that difficult experience was I able to give my Perfectionist the attention, observation, and care that it needed. Now, I can tell just by the physical reactions I have when I'm being drawn into the Perfectionist, and I have strategies for addressing it before I turn to making self-sabotaging decisions.

Our goal is progress, not perfection. I am successful at recognising my Bound Nature before it results in self-sabotage about 90% of the time, and the remaining 10% where I am not quite successful is much less impactful than it would have been 6 months ago. That is major progress.

Adding Deeper Understanding

Bound Nature roles are just the beginning when it comes to mastering our self-sabotaging behaviours. You may remember early in the book, all behaviours stem from thoughts and emotions which stem from beliefs which stem from our early influences. In order to stop our BNs from self-sabotage, we must understand their roots, what needs they once served and what underlying beliefs they are connected to.

Underlying Beliefs

Uncovering our underlying beliefs and challenging them is the ultimate goal of mindset work. This is how we maximise our potential: by releasing ourselves from the stories that have been holding us back.

Every BN is dictated by an underlying belief that no longer serves us. How do we go about uncovering our underlying beliefs? By free-writing about and in our BN. Journaling gives us the separation necessary to see our thoughts and emotions objectively.

When I journal: "There's some guilt, some anxiety about my body being different, and therefore some shame. If I'm not lean (thin), then I'm fat and a slob and I show people that I don't care about myself."

I can take that a step further and finish the thought...If I don't have a perfect body, then what's the point? If I don't have a perfect body, then I'm fat and pathetic. If I don't have a perfect body, then I don't deserve love or success.

Underlying belief: In order to deserve love or success, I have to be perfect.

When I wrote those words more than a year ago, I didn't know that I believed that in order to deserve love or success, I had to be perfect. I had no idea. The immediate reaction I had was that this belief was untrue - I don't actually believe that, but I behave as though I do when I am in Bound Nature.

It was also very clear to me where this underlying belief came from--what it's influences were. As a child, any mistakes were punished with abuse, and so I learned that I had to be perfect if I wanted to be loved.

Using journaling to dig into our subconscious beliefs is challenging. It requires persistence, curiosity, and bravery. So often we get "too close" to the truth and we back away, fearful of what we're digging up. The alternative, however, is far more distressing: we continue to self-sabotage and have no idea why.

Stopping Self-Sabotage

The key in using awareness around Bound Nature to stop self-sabotage is to persistently ask ourselves "why." Why do I eat mindlessly? Why do I need to comfort myself right now? Why does boredom or anxiety or anger lead me to behaving in this way? Why am I so concerned with what other people think of me? Why do I care about this goal over a different one? Why am I so impatient?

Why, why, why. There are reasons for everything we do, say, feel, and believe. Uncover them, own them, and compassionately ask more of yourself.

Once these subconscious beliefs are understood, stopping self-sabotage becomes much like the game Mouse Trap: an intricate puzzle has been put together in our subconscious, leading to a self-sabotaging behaviour, when the plastic mouse is trapped under the falling basket. When we are aware of the emotions, thoughts, and physical sensations that precede the behaviour, we can stop the cycle before the basket cages the mouse. As we practice self-awareness and build on our self-knowledge, we stop the cycle earlier and earlier, until most of the puzzle fails to be built at all.

How To Spend More Time in Free Nature (And Remove The Harmful Bound Nature)

Hey,

It's Tom here - founder of Mindset Rx'd. After reading this fantastic book by Coach Rachel, you're most likely wanting to move forward with your mindset. Well, good news, that's possible, and it's free.

In our free Facebook community, Mindset for Functional Athletes, you will find a group of athletes and coaches who have embarked upon the journey to become the athlete - and person - they know they are possible of becoming. We're a tribe who aren't going to settle for average. We're going to master our mindsets and move forward, relentlessly.

As well as a community which you won't find elsewhere, we also share the tools and strategies we teach athletes to stay on top of their mental-emotional state.

In short, if you want to keep growing as an athlete (and in all the other areas of your life), this is the place to be.

You can find it by searching on Facebook for '**Mindset for Functional Athletes**', or by heading to:
www.mindsetrxd.com/community

Best,

Tom

Printed in Great Britain
by Amazon